IN THE BAG

A year of ready-to-use assemblies for primary school

John Wright

Kevin
Mayhew

First published in 2001 by
KEVIN MAYHEW LTD
Buxhall, Stowmarket, Suffolk IP14 3BW
E-mail: info@kevinmayhewltd.com

9 8 7 6 5 4

ISBN 1 84003 833 0
Catalogue No 1500465

Cover design by Angela Selfe
Edited by Elisabeth Bates
Typeset by Louise Selfe
Printed and bound in Great Britain

Introduction

I'll never forget it. There I was, ordained as a Church of England clergyman just a week, and the Team Rector said, 'You'd better do Thursday's assembly at Sladen, John.'

'Of course,' I said. It was later that I panicked.

What did you *do*? Nothing at Theological College had prepared me for this. I asked my colleagues and other clergy in the area. None was much help. Some even said, 'I've never really known, and I have been doing them for years.'

I bought my way out of trouble the first time – I threw mini-chocolate bars at the children! Fortunately that was the end of the summer term and I had a few weeks to prepare myself. Even so it was two years before each assembly ceased to be a real cause of anxiety beforehand.

I survived, and some teachers have been kind enough to say nice things about some of my assemblies and have even encouraged the preparation of this book. The other great source of encouragement has been the many children I have worked with at assembly. I was surprised to discover some time ago that I enjoyed taking assemblies and the contact it gave me with the children.

The idea behind this book is simple. There are assemblies set out in three terms of ten assemblies, so that you could manage a whole year of weekly assemblies using it. *And* none of the ideas requires massive, advance preparation. (So many assembly books say things like 'Get the children to make a model of the Tower of London in the three weeks before.')

I know many clergy do share my view that assemblies give them an important opportunity to meet with children and tell them about the Christian faith which sustains them. I know that more and more lay people are helping with Christian assemblies in schools. I have also met teachers who would like some extra, but simple, help.

I hope this book may help them all – and perhaps someone else will be saved from my early mixture of panic and ignorance.

John Wright

How to use this book

However you like.

    I have set it out in three terms, beginning with the Autumn Term, to fit the school year. I have assumed a weekly visit and have therefore varied the style and tempo. Some weeks are very active and even noisy. Others are much quieter. I have included some main festivals (Christmas, Holy Week) and some events (Harvest, Christian Aid Week). Sometimes the order will need varying dependent on when particular events occur.

These are the principles underlying what I do:

- I want the children to learn about God and about Jesus – so nearly all assemblies finish on that subject.

- I try to avoid only talking. Usually I bring in one or more objects concealed in a bag.

- Quite often I try to get the children doing things as well as listening and watching.

- Repetition pays. It really does help to reinforce.

Each assembly contains:

- the theme or aim

- any props needed

- a description of the method

- a message

- suggested hymns and prayers. I always end with a prayer and at most schools a hymn or worship song is sung. Most of the hymns are taken from *Kidsource* (Kevin Mayhew, 1999) and these are shown by (KS + number) after the hymn.

Use this book to suit you. You may find the theology too slight or not to your taste. If so, amend the message to suit you and your beliefs. Let the book be a help, a prompt, and an inspiration for better ideas of your own.

Getting to know you

Introducing you – and God

Theme/Aim
This assembly is used at the start of a school year to introduce yourself to children who may not know you and at the same time to encourage the children to take an interest in God. This is done by telling them something about the person facing them.

I tend to start each year with this. The first time it introduces me to everyone. After that there are always some children for whom it is new, and others who help out by remembering – and are very pleased with themselves when they do. At the same time it reinforces what the 'regulars' have learned before.

Props
A miniature cricket bat, a tape (music) and a joke book, all in the bag.

These are my props, but they will be different for everyone. It has to be personal. These are those for a cricket fanatic, who enjoys music and loves silly jokes!

Method
'Hello' is important. Be friendly. Explain to the children, or to the new children, if you have done it before, that you want to tell them something about yourself, and that there are items in the bag which are all to do with things you like.

Then invite them to guess what is in the bag. Response will vary. Sooner or later someone will, for example, guess 'a book'. If they do, take the book out of the bag and say 'What sort of book?' and the usual first answer is a Bible! They never seem to guess a joke book first time out, so eventually you may have to let on that it is a joke book. You could then read out a suitable awful joke.

Sometimes you have to help quite a lot. An example is as follows:

The cricket bat – Why? One child will always say, 'You like cricket', which is quite right. I am fairly hopeless at it. 'Perhaps,' I say sadly, looking at my miniature bat (the sort you collect autographs on) 'I would do better if I used a larger bat . . .'

The tape – Why? After the bat they start to get the hang of it, so one says, 'You like music,' and you can agree that is so.

The joke book – Why? It is easy now. 'You like jokes.' If you do, admitting it will mean some children will tell you jokes if they see you in school.

Once you have identified your three items you ask the whole school these questions in turn.
>   Who likes cricket?
>   Who likes music, even if of a different sort?
>   Who likes silly jokes?

Some will put up their hands to each of these.

Message   Tell the children that they now know more about the leader than they did before you started. You also know a bit more about them. Say that over the weeks to come you want to get to know each other better, and while doing that you also want to help them get to know more about God, because God is the best and most important person to know.

Prayer   I would usually make up a very simple prayer on this occasion. An example is: 'Lord God, help us to get to know you better and to learn to trust you as our friend' and the children saying the 'Amen'.

Hymn   I often allow the hymn to be whatever the music teacher chooses, though some weeks I might ask for a particular hymn. This first week is one where I always simply accept what comes.

This assembly is very simple but it has proved a good way of gaining the confidence of the children by showing them that we all like some of the same things. It also introduces them from the very first week to the idea of thinking about God. The objects vary from leader to leader but the idea behind is the same.

Getting to know each other

Theme/Aim   In Week One the children were introduced to you, the assembly leader, and then directly to the desire that they should get to know God. This week you build on that by trying to show them more that is in common.

Props   None. Just you.

Method   Begin by reminding the children that you introduced yourself the week before. You found that you had a certain amount in common.

'My Christian name is John/Julie, etc. Do we have any other Johns/Julies here?' (John is less popular than it was, so often the answer is NO. Some names will have lots of them. If there are no others, ask if there are any Johns or Julies at home – brothers, sisters, fathers, mothers, uncles, aunts, grandparents, friends . . . There will be some, unless you have a very unusual name.)

Then you can say, 'My wife's name is Elizabeth, though she is usually called Liz.' (More 'Lizs' than 'Johns' but a similar principle applies.)

Then 'My children are Ian and Sarah' and again you try to find some among the children. (Depending on your family, or lack of it, you can use parents' names, friends – it doesn't matter.)

From people move on to animals. 'We have a dog called Sheba. She is a very nice black dog, and she can be very silly.' (This often gets a laugh.) 'Who has a dog at home?' Hands will go up. (Similar for cats. Or, again, parents or other relatives or friends may have a dog or cat.)

Then move on to other animals, making any link you can (e.g. 'We had a hamster once, called Killer?') Rabbits, fish, birds and so on. At each animal ask the children to put up their hands if they have such a creature. Some children will not have any of these, so invite them to tell you what animals they do have at home, or if they have none, that other family, friends or neighbours have.

Warning: This can go on for ever if you let it, as children love talking about animals. You have to stop it some time.

Message   Last week we discovered things we all liked together. This week we have found out that as people we share names in our families, and animals. All of us are different and still we share so much.

   This leads to the point that Jesus was human like us and that had he been here this morning he too would have been able to put his hand up to some of the questions. 'You and I,' you say, 'can be friends because we share a lot. Jesus shares with us, so we can be friends with him too.'

Prayer   The prayer of St Richard seems to be appropriate here.

   Dear Lord, friend and brother,
   May we know you more clearly,
       love you more dearly,
       follow you more nearly.
   Day by day.

Hymn   I suggest either 'Jesus is a friend of mine' (KS 195), 'When Jesus walked in Galilee' or, if you want to use the animal theme, 'All things bright and beautiful' (KS 8).

Learning about God

Theme/Aim The first two weeks have introduced the children to the idea that one gets to know people better over time. This week develops that idea in a visual way.

Props *(In the bag)* One or more jigsaws, preferably with a large box so everyone can see the picture.

Method Take the jigsaw out of the bag. Ask the children what it is. A jigsaw puzzle, of course. How do they work? Someone will explain that you build up the picture slowly by fitting one piece into another. Ideally, more than one child will do the explaining, building up (a bit like a jigsaw) to the fact that when all the pieces are put together correctly the picture can be seen. And what is the picture? It is the one on the box. You could do a jigsaw without the picture but it is much easier if you have it as a guide.

Message Learning to know God is a bit like a jigsaw. It becomes clearer as you learn more. And it is easier if you have a picture to begin with. Jesus is the best picture of God we have, and by seeing what Jesus was like we can find out more about God.

Prayer God our Father,
    you sent Jesus to live among us and to teach us your ways;
    help us to know you better because of Jesus
    and to live as you would want.
God our Father,
Amen.

Hymn 'Who put the colours in the rainbow?' (KS 386) or 'Father God, I wonder' (KS 52).

Harvest – the brick

Note: Weeks may need rearranging to fit in with Harvest. Many schools have a special for Harvest where parents attend. This seems to go well at such a service/assembly.

Theme/Aim   The intention, very conventional for Harvest, is to use the occasion to emphasise the greatness of creation, and the abundance of it. However, it is done in a rather unconventional way, surprising the children with something they may not think of as part of 'God's creation'.

Props   *(In the bag)* A brick wrapped in a carrier bag, sufficiently covered and padded that nothing other than its weight can be deduced.

Method   (This usually takes place against a background of harvest offerings, which gives a real contrast. It still works without this advantage.)

You begin by announcing to the children that you have in the bag something from your/a garden, a statement which should be true! Enquire what they think it is.

All sorts of guesses follow. A cauliflower. A marrow. Or whatever. Then get one of them to hold it. They discover it is very heavy. More guesses are made. It can even be passed around provided it is wrapped up sufficiently well to remain concealed.

Usually no one guesses correctly. (If a child does guess correctly, unwrap the brick and say, 'Well done'. You can't win them all!) Keep it going for a while until the time comes when it is the moment to have a look.

One of the children should be asked to come up and unwrap it. 'Be careful,' you say, helpfully. 'You do not want to break it.' Finally it is revealed – a *brick*! The children laugh (as did a British Legion Harvest Home when it was used on them). I have even known the teachers smile!

Message   The children think it is a joke until it is explained. The brick does indeed come from the garden – you never said it was growing there. *But* it is made from clay and other natural ingredients, all of them put there by God.

Point out how many people are involved in creating the brick:

- Someone has to dig the materials out of the ground.

- Someone else looks after the machine which creates the brick shape.

- Someone else sees that the brick is cooked in a big oven.

- Someone else sells the bricks, another sends them where they are needed and yet another uses them to build the houses.

Finally the brick helps us to be sheltered, warm and dry.

The brick is as much a gift of God as crops and vegetables. Our enjoyment of it depends, like them, on us all playing our part to make good use of what God has given us. God gives us everything. It is up to us to make good use of it.

Prayer   Lord God,
    help us to see you in everything you have made,
    in obvious things like food and water,
    and the less obvious things such as materials we turn into
    products for our use.
Teach us to use all we have unselfishly,
    so that others may benefit as well,
    and most of all, give us thankful hearts. Amen.

Hymn   There are lots of harvest hymns. 'For the beauty of the earth' is quite good here with its verse beginning 'For each perfect gift of thine'. Another with good words is 'Harvest time' (KS 95).

The Great Commandment
The Peace

Theme/Aim
- To build on the 'friendship' theme in the first two assemblies of the term and to use this as a way of introducing the children to the 'Great Commandment'.
- To introduce the children to the 'Peace' used in many churches, so that a little more of what goes on is shown to them; should they go to church at any time, they will be more at ease with what's going on because they will know about that part of the service.

Props
None.

Method
Start by saying: 'Christians are people who regard Jesus as their friend and they try to use Jesus' life as the example of how to live.' Then tell them that although that might sound very hard to do, Jesus helped us by summing up his teaching in what is sometimes known as the Great Commandment. He told them to:

'Love God and love one another.'

This means putting God first, to recognise that God is the most important thing anywhere ever, and then to look after each other. (You may care to give the Great Commandment in a fuller form, and to explain it in a more detailed way.)

Once this has been explained to them, go on to tell them about the Peace. Christians do this to show their intention to be at peace with each other and friends with each other, especially before they receive Communion in which they remember Jesus' last meal with his friends.

After this, show them one version of the Peace which is used in some churches, where everybody present links hands with each other.

All the children are gathered into one big circle. All hold hands and the leader says, 'The peace of the Lord be always with you', and they reply, 'And also with you.' Then, without breaking the circle, they turn to the two next to them (in turn) and shaking the hand up and down say, 'Peace be with you.' (This can be turned into a 'Mexican Wave' of peace, or a 'Peace Ripple' by the leader shaking hands with the one on the right, who then does it to the one on his/her right, and so on until it gets round the full circle. This is fun but it works best with children of 7 and over. 5s and 6s find it hard to keep going.)

A rather nice refinement was discovered on one occasion when a child came in after we had begun. We opened the circle to bring him in and made the excellent Christian point that no one is excluded. There is always room for one more. (Or you could include a teacher who has been watching.)

It is quite good to do the sharing of the peace a second time anyway, as a reinforcement.

Message   The message is contained in the method. Extra words seem to be unnecessary.

Prayer   May God's peace fill our lives and make us friends with each other. Amen.

Hymn   'Let there be peace on earth' or 'Give me oil in my lamp (KS 66) or 'Make me a channel of your peace' (KS 248) or lots of others on the theme.

The two teddy bears

Theme/Aim   To encourage the children to see that it is possible to love and care about a variety of people regardless of their abilities or what they look like. In recent years this week has coincided with television's 'Children in Need' appeal whose emblem is a teddy bear with a patch over one eye.

Props   *(In the bag – or a suitcase)* Two teddy bears, one which looks very old and battered and one much newer, smarter bear.

Method   Both bears are in a large bag, or suitcase. Ask, 'What's in the bag?' and they have a few guesses where you can pretend to look in the bag to see if they are right. Eventually, either someone guesses right or you say, 'I will show you'.

First out is the newer teddy bear. Lots of 'ah's. 'He is rather nice, isn't he?' Put 'him' on a chair, bench, or shelf so he can be seen.

And then pull out the old bear. He usually gets an even bigger response. (In the author's case the children are told that he is my first bear and that he is nearly as old as me. They are shown how his fur has nearly worn off, 'cuddled away' over the years, and where his ear had to be sewn on again – because I used to carry him around by the ear and it came off. . . . Every bear is different – but every old bear has a history!) He is placed next to his colleague.

The next question is, 'Which do you think I love the most – the old and rather tatty bear or the smart new one?' So far they have always said 'the old one' which demonstrates that children get the point very easily. And they are quite right. The old bear is the most loved – he and his owner have been together a long time. (But the other one is loved too, because bears are nearly always presents and they carry the love of the person who gave them.)

Message   The teddy bears are very clever because they only do one thing but they do it brilliantly. They help spread love. They receive it, and manage to give it back. They do that regardless of what they look like. Age is no drawback and neither is looking odd, being damaged, or even having something missing.

It is true of teddy bears and it is also true of people. Everyone is capable of love, whatever they look like, regardless of what they can do. God loves us all and cares about us, different as we are. 'Some are like you children, fresh and new; others (like the leader) are older and more battered. God loves us all.'

And God also wants us to be like that to each other.

Prayer

Dear God,
    you love every one of us, different though we are.
Help us to care for each other,
    regardless of how we look or what we can do, and in particular
    to look after children less fortunate than ourselves.
Amen.

or

God our Father,
    your Son Jesus showed his love for the people he met
    by healing them when they needed it.
Teach us that Jesus will still help us if we ask him
    because he loves us too.
Amen.

Hymn

'Jesus' love is very wonderful' (KS 208) or 'Can we love one another' (KS 22).

Story time

Theme/Aim   It is good to slow things down occasionally. Some of the assemblies can be quite noisy, or use strange props. It is important that the children are ready to listen sometimes, so you can pass on some of the message directly.

Reading a story once in a while helps them to be ready to listen at other times. That is the theory, and it seems to work. In any case, as with any form of speaking in public, a change of style and tempo is useful.

Props   *(In the bag)* The book or magazine from which to read. Some find it easier to read from something rather than trust to memory, though you can often embellish it a little. If you are happier without such a 'prop' it is up to you. Do it the way you feel most comfortable.

Method   Each to their own. It can be useful to ask the children what they have to do if there is a story to be read. The answer comes, 'sit quietly' and 'listen' (or it always has so far!) and there is then a much better chance they will do it.

THE STORY

Message   This will depend on the story. Good stories often require very little addition.

One suggestion might be the story of Jairus' Daughter (Mark 5:21-24, 35-42) read from an easy version of the Bible, such as the Good News Bible. The story of a sick child fits in well with the week before. A non-religious story which would fit is that of the *Velveteen Rabbit.*

Many assembly leaders use stories which feature the same character. The author uses a series about a mouse and takes in a toy mouse, dressed as a member of the clergy, which is enormously popular.

Prayer   This rather depends on the story, or you might want to make up your own. If the story is of help or healing, either of the prayers at the end of last week (Autumn Six) is appropriate.

Hymn   As with the prayer, the hymn depends on the story. For once, why not sing one of the children's favourites? They will be quite happy to tell you which they are! Or ask the teacher in charge of hymn practice.

Christingle

Lots of churches have a Christingle Service at some time in the year, many of those services being at the beginning of Advent. Some schools have them as well. If you can use the assembly before it happens it will encourage attendance. If afterwards, you can build on what has been done. If your area does not hold such a service, you can still use the Christingle and explain what others do.

Theme/Aim

The Christingle is used as a visual aid. It tells its own story (which is probably why the service is so popular).

Props

(In the bag – but beware of the sticks!) One Christingle, fully prepared. (Plus matches or a lighter.) The Christingle consists of an orange, with a red band around it, a candle coming out of it, and four sticks with nuts and raisins on.

Method

Produce the Christingle from the bag carefully as it is a bit spiky. 'Does anyone know what it is?' It is possible that in the first year this will have to be explained but if you repeat it each year some children will remember in later years. Some may have attended a service.

'It is a Christingle.' You light it, and then explain the components of it, or, even better, get the children to tell you.

The orange is the world, which God made.

The four sticks are the four seasons of the year or, in a rather nice variation, North, South, East and West.

The fruits and sweets represent God's goodness in providing all the good things we need. (One variation is to have a jelly baby on one of the sticks. This stands for the people of the world – and is enormously popular with the consumers after a real Christingle service.)

The red ribbon around the orange tells us of God's love for the world which is shown by the blood of Jesus who died for us. As the ribbon surrounds the orange so God's love surrounds us all.

The lighted candle is Jesus, the Light of the World.

Message   The message is in the method. If there is a Service shortly to be held, encourage them to go.

Prayer   One from the Christingle Service is useful. Alternatively a prayer thanking God for his care and his love in sending us Jesus is appropriate.

Dear God
Thank you for making our world and for sending us Jesus
   to love us and care for us.
Teach us that the best way to thank you
   is to look after your world and the people on it.
For Jesus' sake.
Amen.

Hymn   It is ideal to sing one of the hymns which are often sung at the service. 'Shine, Jesus, shine' (KS 237) or 'This little light of mine' (KS 343) or 'God's love is like a circle' are all suitable and are known to have been used at Christingle Services. 'Can you see what we have made' (KS 24) is a specifically Christingle hymn where the words reinforce the message.

Who is the vicar?

Note: This assembly works because the clergy have distinctive clothing. If you are clergy or a minister you can do it yourself. If not, can you persuade one to come in and help?

Theme/Aim
There are two main aims. The first is to show the children that you should not judge people by appearances alone. You should see what they say and do and see if it is consistent. The second is to demonstrate that if you do base your opinion on what a person says and does it leads you to see that Jesus is the one to follow.

Props
A suitcase (*not a bag*) containing a set of clergy robes depending on the minister and church. A spare clerical collar plus something to fix it with (a paper clip is very useful). A spare set of robes is useful, but it can be done without.

Method
Begin by asking the children a question. 'How do you know that I am/he/she is a minister?' Usually – though it may need prompting – one of them says, 'That thing round your neck'. (The collar is essential on this occasion.)

'Wait a moment,' you say. Undo the case and robe in front of them. 'Does that make me a vicar/minister?' 'Y-E-S' they say (they do, really). 'So . . .' you say, as if inspiration has just struck, 'I have an idea.' Will Mrs Smith/Mr Jones help me?' (Choose one of the staff whom you have briefed just before assembly.)

Then dress them like the minister. If you do not have a spare set of robes available you or the minister take off your robes and put them on the other person. When it is done, amid great laughter, say 'There is something missing . . . of course, the collar.' Get out a spare and fasten it with a paper clip.

Message   Has Mrs Smith/Mr Jones become a vicar? No, of course not, the children can see that at once.

Ask them how they know. They will say that they *know* Mrs Smith/Mr Jones is a teacher. (They may know the minister too. They know they are who they are, not just because of the clothes but because of what they do.)

The message is that you should not judge by appearances. You test what a person looks like with all you know or find out about them and thinking about what they say, or do, or are.

The conclusion is that they should apply the same test to Jesus. Find out what he said he was, what he did, and said, and the life he led. 'If you do that, I think you will find out for yourself that Jesus is the person you should most want to know and be like.'

Prayer   Lord God,
Father of Jesus and of each one of us,
     give us the desire to want to know more about Jesus and what he said and did, so that as we learn more we can try to live more and more the way he wants us to.
Amen.

Hymn   'A man there lived in Galilee'. 'Jesus rode a donkey into town' (KS 212) contrasts what one sees with what happens, and 'Who spoke words of wisdom and life' (KS 387).

Warning: This assembly seems to generate a great deal of laughter from the children. The 'vicar' needs to know the children a certain amount for it to be done at all.

Jesus – the best present

Theme/Aim   Children often seem to associate Christmas with the presents they are going to get, so this assembly is intended to make them think about Jesus, and the real point of Christmas.

Props   (In the bag) A present you have received which is small and of no great monetary value but which is special because of the person or reason it was given. The author uses a cheap toy called a 'Play-a-Tune Computer' which caught his eye in a shop and made him laugh, so one of the family bought it for him without telling him. Anything will do, as long as the value is in its being given, not in itself.

Method   Ask the children what they want for Christmas. There will be a deluge of answers, and many of the things will be quite expensive (and some of them they know they will get!).

When you have had enough answers, ask them if they can guess one of the best presents you have ever had. After a few guesses show them it. At first, because it is a lesser item, they may be disappointed. So you explain that it was bought for you/made for you, with love, by your wife, child, brother, friend. It is special for that reason. Love makes it valuable.

Message   The best Christmas present ever was Jesus. Jesus is God's gift to us, not because we have earned it, but out of love.

Tell the children you hope they receive everything they want, and their families can afford, for Christmas but to remember, in the excitement, that Jesus is the best Christmas present ever, and to find time on Christmas Day to say 'Thank you, God, for Jesus.'

Prayer   Father God,
we thank you for the first and best Christmas present ever,
your Son Jesus Christ.
As we enjoy Christmas,
may we remember those who will not,
and try to help those less lucky than us,
because Jesus came for us all.
Amen.

Hymn   Nearly all carols are appropriate, as are 'See him lying on a bed of straw' (KS 291) or 'As with gladness' (KS 14) (if you don't mind an early Epiphany).

Note: This assembly could be used as effectively in the first week after the holidays as it will be around Epiphany and could tie in with the Wise Men and their 'presents'.

Don't put Jesus away with the decorations

Theme/Aim   To show the children that Jesus is important all the time and not just at Christmas, at a time when the world is returning to 'normal'.

Props   *(In the bag)* A Christmas card, a Christmas decoration, and a present.

Method   (This is ideally done just after Twelfth Night when all the decorations have come down.)

Ask the children, 'I wonder what is in the bag?' Take out the items. What might it be about? Someone will say 'Christmas', and they are quite right. If it is after Twelfth Night you could ask if their decorations are still up. Or you could say, 'We have taken our decorations down/will take them down on Friday.' Remind them that all the decorations are packed away and put in a box in the roof, or the garage, or a cupboard – out of sight.

Ask them why we do this. Either they will say, or you can tell them, 'Because Christmas is over.' We will not need them until next December.

Message   Lots of people seem to make the effort to be nicer at Christmas, but seem to forget very soon after. We visit elderly relatives, for instance, and can often forget the rest of the year. It is as if the special goodness and love of Jesus is only for once a year.

We know better. We celebrate Jesus' birthday once a year, but his birth and all he was and did is for every day.

Don't pack him away and forget him until next year!

Prayer   Father God,

once a year we celebrate the birth of Jesus, your Son;

help us to see that his is the best way for every day,

and to know and trust him all year long.

Amen.

Hymn   Any Christmas carol (a final airing for the year?) or 'We three kings' or 'I love the lights on Christmas trees' (KS 137).

Story time –
the sick brought to Jesus

SPRING TERM: WEEK 2

The next two weeks' assemblies develop a theme of trust. This week's assembly is designed to be quieter in anticipation of the relative chaos of Week Three, to which it links fairly directly.

Theme/Aim   To develop the theme of trust, and to read one of the Bible stories about Jesus to the children.

Props   *(In the bag)* A Bible (or this book).

Method   *(Story)* The story to be used should be one which involves the sick person being dependent on their friends. Two of the best are Mark 8:22-25 (Jesus healing a blind man at Bethsaida) or Mark 10:46-52 (Jesus heals blind Bartimaeus) where others help – the first is the best of these. Mark 2:1-12 (Jesus heals a paralysed man whose friends lower him from the roof) is excellent for the help, but links less well than the blindness with next week. It is such a good story, through, that this may not matter.

Message   The stories do most of the work for you. Remind the children that other people helped the sick person, and that God looked after them and healed them, through Jesus.

Prayer   Lord,
    we know you love us and will look after us.
Teach us to trust you,
    and that, whatever happens, you will be with us.
Amen.

Hymn   'Jesus' hands were kind hands' (KS 194).

Trust in others, trust in God

This assembly continues the theme of trust present last week.

Theme/Aim

The aim is to demonstrate in a dramatic way how we may need to trust others and how if we do so it works. The same principle applies to our being prepared to trust God.

Props

None – or the leader and five volunteers.

Method

Remind the children of last week's story, either by getting them to tell you, or, if that fails, telling them the outline again.

You now need two volunteers who are friends. Produce a blindfold and blindfold one of them. Then organise an obstacle course, using chairs, people or objects depending on where you are. The sighted one takes their 'blind' friend and leads them through the obstacles by hand. When they have done it successfully they stand at the front together.

A further pair are called for and one of them, again, is blindfolded. They are told to negotiate the course as before. This time, however, they must not touch. The leader directs by voice alone, using only the five instructions: *forward – back – right – left – stop*. This is more difficult, as sometimes the need to stop is forgotten, but in the end and amidst some laughter the task is accomplished.

Finally, a lone volunteer is requested. Their partner, who is blindfolded, is *the leader* . . . more laughter usually, but the job is completed.

Message

The five who have helped are often a help in drawing out the message. The two to be blindfolded will usually agree how odd it felt. The three who led will usually say that they were trying to keep their partners safe.

It is all about trust. The three blindfolded can only manage with help but friends can be trusted to help them, like the man in last week's story whose friends helped him before he was healed. There will be times in life when we are 'in the dark' and are not sure what to do. When that happens God can always be trusted to help us find our way. Our friends could be trusted. God can be trusted even more.

Prayer You could perhaps repeat whatever prayer you used last week to help reinforce the point.

or

Help us, Lord,
   to trust you to take us through life and to be there for us whenever we need you.
In the name of Jesus.
Amen.

Hymn 'I'm putting my hand in your hand now' (KS 158).

Prayer

Of all the assemblies suggested in this book this one is probably the most dependent on the individual presenting it. A basic approach is set out but every leader will vary it in some way.

Theme/Aim

The last two weeks have all been about 'trust', with last week focusing on 'trusting God'. This week builds upon that and leads into prayer, our way of communicating with the God we trust.

Props

(In the bag) The picture of the praying hands is very good or other pictures could be used, or perhaps a hassock from out of church, if your church has them. You could use a pair of bicycle clips (see Method).

Method

'I want to show you something.' From out of the bag take the picture and hold it up for the children to see. If it is just a class or at a small school pass it round. Then ask (assuming it is the hands) 'What is it a picture *of* ?'. Someone will say, usually, or tell them if not, 'Praying'. If you use the bicycle clips say, 'This is to do with praying.' They may be intrigued . . .

The next question is 'What is praying?' The answer will come, 'Talking to God.' 'Yes,' you say, 'and there is something else too.' They usually try quite hard – 'Asking for things', 'Saying sorry' are examples. The right answer is, 'You have to listen as well as talk', but you will probably have to supply it (most adults might not get it either).

This is followed by, 'How do you pray?' and the answer comes back so often 'Hands together, eyes closed'! 'Where and when do you pray?' receives lots of answers and there are lots of possible answers, so church, assembly, in your bedroom could all be offered. The answer you are searching for with these two questions, and which you may have to supply, is *anyhow, anywhere* and *any time.*

Message

Prayer is being in touch with God. You can do it any time you feel like it, anywhere you are. Putting your hands together and closing your eyes is fine most of the time – it stops you being distracted and helps you concentrate. Tell them of people who pray when walking the dog. Ask them, 'Do you think they put their hands together and close their eyes?' They laugh and say *no*.

Now suggest you can do it any time you need to – even when out riding your bicycle. But if you do it then, I wouldn't close my eyes and put my hands together, would you?

Tell God anything, *and* be prepared to listen. You probably won't hear a voice but if you do listen you will find that you begin to know what to do, or find you can somehow cope better. Repeat 'Tell God and be prepared to listen.' Then finish with 'Let us do it now – think very hard of something you would like to share with God and, to help us concentrate better we will all put our hands together and close our eyes.' And they do.

Prayer Use the Lord's Prayer, saying it a line at a time and getting the children to repeat it after you. This helps the children who do not know it very well.

Hymn The Caribbean version of the Lord's Prayer might be useful, or 'Dear Lord, my Father who's in heaven' (KS 36). Others which would be appropriate are 'Father, I place into your hands' or 'What a friend we have in Jesus' or 'There are hundreds of sparrows, thousands, millions' (KS 320).

Jesus says

SPRING TERM: WEEK 5

Theme/Aim   The idea is to use a game the children may well have played to get them to think about using Jesus as an example for what they do.

Props   None – or, if you like, everybody present!

Method   Begin by asking the children if any of them have played the game 'Simon Says', also known as 'O'Grady Says' (and probably other '. . . Says', as well). Some, probably most, will have done so. However, to refresh our memories and to teach those who don't know it, we play the game. The children all stand.

The Leader (you) gives out instructions such as 'lift your right hand', and then does it. The children *only* obey if you say 'Simon Says – Lift your right hand.' Without the words 'Simon Says' they should ignore the instruction. A whole range of simple movements can be done, and they can only change position in response to 'Simon Says'.

Those who get it wrong are eliminated (it is best to make them sit down). Lots will get it wrong the first time so you then announce that it was only a 'practice', so everyone has at least two goes. The trick as leader is to go faster as it progresses, for instance, follow a series of quick fire 'Simon Says' with a command without it.

Some children are very good at this, so it can go on quite a long time. You may well decide you have made your point without eliminating them all.

Message   In the game the instructions to follow are the ones 'Simon' gives.

In life, for Christians, the instructions to follow are the ones Jesus gives. You find these instructions in the stories about Jesus in the Bible, through the Church, and in the lives of real Christians. All of it depends on looking to Jesus and doing as he says.

Jesus says, rather than Simon Says.

Prayer   Father God,
          help us to follow Jesus at all times, hearing what he says,
          and doing what he tells us, so that our lives
          and those of the people we live with will be happier.
          Amen.

Hymn   'I want to be like Jesus' (KS 181) or 'Be the centre of my life,
          Lord Jesus' (KS 20).

God's rules

Theme/Aim   The idea is to build on ideas of trust and to encourage the children to 'obey God's rules' using the Great Commandment (see Autumn Term: Week Five).

Props   *(In the bag)* These will vary for each person. A set of rules for a club, a British Legion or any other organisation will do, plus the instruction book for a word processor, audio-recorder, camera, etc. If the school has a set of rules, however simple, these could be used.

Method   Begin by asking about rules and instructions. What are they for? This part will vary from school to school but themes will recur.

- To keep us safe.

- To help us to do things.

- To show us what can be done (or can't).

- To help us live and work together.

Then produce the props. The rules of any organisation explain usually who can be a member, what you have to do as a member, and what is allowed. At the same time, we learn who is in charge.

The instructions for the machine do two things. They enable us to use all the clever devices programmed in it – or they would. (It can be ages before you find some of them because lots of us don't bother to read the book.) And it helps you out when things go wrong so they can be put right.

Laws in a country or a school help us to live more pleasantly with each other and to get the best from life – or they should!

Message   Life needs some rules too. We need guidance to get the most enjoyment for ourselves, so as not to spoil things for others and to sort ourselves out when we go wrong. Jesus gave us two basic rules: 'Love God and love each other.' God ought always to be recognised by us as the one who always looks after us, and who should matter most *and* we ought to look after each other.

God is in charge and if we remember that and look after each other life will work better. Remember – live by God's rules, and you will not go far wrong.

Prayer   One possibility would be to repeat Spring Term: Week Five –
'Jesus Says'.

Hymn   'If I were a butterfly' (KS 128) or 'When I needed a neighbour'
or 'I can do all things' (KS 124).

Lent – stop something, start something

This assembly needs to be done within a few days of Shrove Tuesday/ Ash Wednesday.

Theme/Aim   The intention is to tell the children something about Lent, and to use that to encourage them to make an effort in Lent to behave better. The concept of voluntarily doing without something is regarded as very strange by most children these days!

Props   *(In the bag)* A frying pan and one packet of sweets or biscuits or something else nice.

Method   Hold up the bag and remove the frying pan. Has anyone any idea what it is about? (It is probably better if Shrove Tuesday has just been rather than still to come.) With luck someone will say 'Pancake Day'! If not, the children have to be told.

The next stage is to ask if anyone knows why we have Pancake Day. No one ever seems to know the real reason so you have to explain that it was the last day before Lent. In Lent people lived very simply with no rich food at all, so on Shrove Tuesday they used to eat up all the rich food before Lent began the next day, which is Ash Wednesday.

You have to make your own judgement on how much you tell the children about Lent. You might tell them that Lent is a period of 40 days, not including Sundays, before Easter; and that during Lent almost everyone used to observe it by living very simply; and that even now some people do 'keep Lent' by giving something up – at which point produce the biscuits, sweets or whatever as an example.

Message   'Why do we do this?' you ask them. The best answer is that it is for us to be a bit more like Jesus, who, according to the Gospels, spent 40 days in the desert without much to eat, so he could think and pray and see what to do.

We all need times when we, too,

- need to think;
- need to recognise that nice things like sweets or biscuits or videos are a blessing not a need;

- need to try and look at our life and see if we need to change.

Say cheerfully 'I am not going to try and make you give up sweets for Lent – unless you want to.' (The children always seem very pleased about that.) 'I do have two things I want you to do for me, or rather one thing to stop doing and one thing to start.'

Stop doing something you know is wrong – like being horrible to your brother or sister.

Start doing something you know you should do – like listening to your teacher or being helpful to your mum.

'Come on,' you urge, 'will you try?' And amazingly lots of them will say *yes*.

Prayer

God, our Father,
  we know we do things we should not do,
  and forget to do good things we could do:
  encourage us in the weeks before Easter
  to become better people, by giving up bad habits
  and taking up good ones.
In the name of Jesus.
Amen.

Hymn

Lent is difficult. Few schools use 'Forty days and forty nights' or want to. One possibility is the Pete Seager hymn based on Ecclesiastes 3, 'To ev'rything, turn, turn, turn'. Another is 'Seek ye first the kingdom of God' (KS 292) or 'Be still, for the presence of the Lord' (KS 19).

Train ticket

Note: This is very noisy. Be ready to be nice to the teaching staff who have to look after the children after you have worked them up.

Theme/Aim
A major part of the thinking behind this one is simply to have fun. It is quite good if the children are never entirely sure what you will come up with – but it might just be good!

The 'proper' aim is to make the point that faith is not only about saying you believe or agree but that it requires action as well.

Prop
(In the bag) A train ticket – but if you don't have one, create one with a postcard.

Method
The first question is 'Which of you has been on a train?' Lots have. Have any been on a steam train? Some will almost certainly have done so. Then you tell them that *they* are going to be a train.

You explain that they are going to line up outside the hall/room (in which assembly takes place) in single file, and then as they come through the door into the hall/room they are to make a 'woo-woo' noise like a train whistle. If the geography of the school permits, you can go out of the hall, round the back and in again – and they can make the noise *twice*. This is, as was said at the head of the page, extremely noisy – and the children have a splendid time.

Only one person does not do it – you, the leader. When they get back you ask them where they have been and they will tell you they have been a train. 'You have been on a journey?' you inquire and they say 'Yes', usually rather loudly.

You then say rather sadly that you didn't go, because you did not get on the train. Show them your ticket and add, 'Look, I've even got my ticket here.' If you think the staff can stand it being done twice you can then repeat it with you somewhere in the middle of the train. (You have to judge whether to do this, or if it is better to calm them down.)

The point is that it is not enough to buy a ticket. You also have to get on the train.

Message	It is the same with a faith, such as Christianity, as it is with a train journey. You do not go anywhere if you buy a ticket and never get on the train. It is equally the case that it is no use saying you believe, or even deciding in your head that it is true, if you never do anything about it. If you believe, it has to result in action, in the way you behave and in being with others who do the same. You could call Baptism the train ticket of faith but you have to do something with the ticket.

Prayer	A simple prayer of personal commitment seems to be appropriate.

Teach us, good Lord,
    that it is not enough to say we believe,
    but that it must be seen in everything we say and do.
Help us to do this, in the way and the name of Jesus.
Amen.

Hymn	'The journey of life' or 'One more step' (KS 273).

Final note: This has been done with twenty-odd children and with nearly one hundred. It may need rearranging for a larger school, perhaps by making them stand up and sit down in a sort of 'mexican wave' rather than physically moving them in and out of the hall.

The Gospels – the light of Jesus

Theme/Aim   The aim is to introduce some of the children to the Gospels, for there are many these days who have almost no idea about them, and to explain that they are four pictures of Jesus, but all are based on the one person. There are not four Jesuses but one.

Props   *(In the bag)* One large candle, preferably the Paschal Candle from church, if you use one and can borrow it, or a large candle on a stand, which can be sited prominently in the middle of the room.

Four other candles which are suitable for being carried. It is ideal if they can be of different sizes and/or colours. If they must be the same size and colour, a different coloured ribbon will make them different.

Method   Light the large candle. If you have done an assembly using candles before (such as Autumn Eight – Christingle) it is usually safe to ask 'What, or who, do you think the candle might represent?' It will probably work even if you haven't done anything like it before. Sometimes the answer will come at once, and sometimes only after prompting, 'Jesus'. So it is.

Then ask for four volunteers. Take the four candles out of the bag and ask the four children to light them from the central candle. The volunteers take their candles to different parts of the room or hall and then you ask the children to turn and look at the one nearest them, and after that to face the front again. What do they think it is all about, you ask. Why four candles, and the moving around? Each class, or school, will respond differently. Some may see the point at once, and some may need it explaining in detail.

Message   If you are lucky you may only have to reinforce what the children tell you, but if not you may have to do nearly all the work for them. This is the message.

The central candle is Jesus. His light is for us all, an example and a way to be. The Bible has four special books which tell us about Jesus when he could be seen on earth. These are called 'Gospels' and they carry the names of Matthew, Mark, Luke and John. They are all different and we see Jesus just a little differently in each – but it is still the same Jesus. The four candles are the

Gospels. When they were first written people only knew about one Gospel so just as the children all turned to look at the nearest candle so they only had the one light of Jesus to see. However, all the Gospels are about the one Jesus in the same way the candles all come from the one central light.

Prayer

God our Father,
 you have given us everything we need,
 and most of all you gave us Jesus to be our light,
 the light of truth.
Help us to be children of light
 and to live by the example of Jesus,
 so that the world may be as good as you always meant it to be.
Amen.

Hymn

'Shine, Jesus, shine' (KS 237) is always popular or 'I'm gonna shine, shine, shine' (KS 152) or the hymn 'We have a Gospel to proclaim'.

Choose the real thing

This should be the last assembly before the end of term.

Theme/Aim This assembly uses the secular symbol of Easter, the Easter Egg, to remind the children that Easter is about Jesus.

Props *(In the bag)* An Easter Egg – as large as possible, and hollow.

Method Hold up the bag, and say, 'I have something in my bag to do with Easter. What do you think it is?' It will probably not be long before one of the children says 'An Easter Egg' – and you agree and produce it.

Lots of people think Easter is not about Jesus at all, you say, but about chocolate eggs like this one. They are wrong. Easter is about Jesus, a real person, who was killed on Good Friday and whom Christians believed was raised to life again on the Sunday.

As for the egg, you add, look at it. It is very nice of course but:

- When you break it (as you then do) it is hollow inside.

- It does not last – not in our house, it doesn't!

Message The Easter Egg has nothing inside and will be gone within a few days. Jesus is always full – of love for us – and lasts for ever.

Enjoy your eggs – but choose the real thing, which is Jesus.

Prayer God our Father,
we find it hard to understand
why Jesus had to die on Good Friday,
when all he said and did was good.
Help us to see that not even death
could end the love and goodness he showed us,
and that the Resurrection is the proof
that he and love and goodness
are with us for ever.
Amen.

Hymn 'Make way' (KS 249) continues the Palm Sunday theme. 'Lord of the dance' is very good at setting Easter in context, as is 'From heaven you came' (KS 62).

Getting close to Jesus

Theme/Aim

This is the first assembly after Easter. Clergy or laity with churches which have a Paschal Candle which has come into Church on Easter Eve should use it if they can. It is a highly visible prop! The intention is to:

- stress the idea of Jesus as the 'Light of the World' and
- encourage the children to get to know Jesus better so that they can 'be set alight' by him.

Props

Paschal Candle and Holder. If your church does not have one, or you cannot borrow it, use a large candle set on a stand. In either case place the candle where the children can walk past it.

Method

Start by explaining about the Paschal Candle. To some extent this can be done by question and answer ('What is this?' 'A candle.' 'What sort of candle?' You may get lucky and find a child who goes to church and knows about it or has seen it at a Baptism) and part may be done by telling them. (This partly depends on whether you have a Paschal Candle or not.)

Tell the children about Paschal Candles coming into church on Easter Eve; about how it comes into a dark church signifying the light of Jesus which was *not* extinguished by the Crucifixion, and about how candles in many churches are given out at Baptism lit from the Paschal Candle, every child baptised receiving their own portion of the light of Jesus.

Light the Paschal Candle or ask one of the children to help you do it. Once that is done all the children are asked to stand. When they have done so ask them, 'If I want you to be a candle what will you need to do?' The answer required, and sometimes offered, is to put their hands together above their heads. (Yes, sometimes you do have to give some hints, but not always.) It is then fairly easy to persuade them to rub their hands up and down above their heads to indicate the flicker of a candle burning.

The (Paschal) Candle needs to be placed somewhere with a lot of room because the whole school is then invited to walk past the candle in single file. As soon as they come alongside the candle the children put their hands above their heads and become candles burning. They keep that going until they have all passed by the candle and are back in their places. Then they can stop, and sit down.

Message   We can 'catch fire' by coming close to Jesus. To be a Christian is to want to know Jesus better. As we get closer to him so we too receive his light for ourselves (as with the Baptism candle) and we should also be visible to others as little lights of Jesus.

Prayer   Lord Jesus,
  light up our lives, and as you are light for us in our lives,
  may we show that same light to those around us.
In your name.
Amen.

Hymn   'Shine, Jesus, shine' (KS 237) or 'Give me oil in my lamp' (KS 66).

God can know us

Theme/Aim   The aim is to show the children that God can care for us and about us in spite of there being so many of us.

Props   None. Or, if you prefer, the leader, one class teacher and one headteacher (you will need to check that the headteacher will be present).

Method   (This varies a little depending on how long the leader has been in a place and how well she/he knows the children.)

The children are reminded that one of the things said at the start of the year was that it would be good if they got to know God, and to trust God, and to treat God as a friend. (For example Autumn Term: Week One.) Then say, 'But aren't there an awful lot of us for God to know each one of us?' adding quickly 'Let's try an experiment'.

First – Explain that you know some of them by name and some you do not. If there is a group such as members of the church choir or Brownies, get them to stand up – they don't seem to mind – as an example of some known to the leader. If you know hardly any, say so. Children respect honesty.

Second – Turn to one of the class teachers, preferably having agreed it with them just before beginning, and ask if she/he knows every child in her/his class. She/he does, of course. So make the whole class stand up; there will probably be more children than the leader knew.

Third – Turn to the Head and ask if she/he knows every child in the school. 'Yes' she/he says, unless she/he is very new, or it is a very large school. A good way to prove it is to go among the children, picking at random and getting them to stand to be identified by the Head. (Headteachers are very good indeed at knowing their children.)

Message   It is possible for humans to know quite large numbers of people. And the Head will not just know the names, she/he will actually know the children to the extent of knowing what they are like and something about them. (This usually prompts the odd smile and the odd worried look when you say this.)

God is greater than any human – even the Head! So it *is* possible for God to know us all and care about us, and we can know God better and find a support and a friend.

Prayer   St Richard's prayer (Autumn Term: Week Two)

Dear Lord, friend and brother
May we know you more clearly,
    love you more dearly,
    follow you more nearly,
Day by day.
Amen.

Hymn   'There are hundreds of sparrows, thousands, millions (God knows me)' (KS 320) might have been written with this in mind.

Note: Obviously the week varies a bit in terms of its place in the summer term. It has been assumed to fall in Week Three.

Theme/Aim   The aim is to draw attention to Christian Aid Week, to help the children recognise that the problems of 'far-off places' *is* something to do with us – and to link this in with the Christian message.

Props   *(In the bag)* Depends on the number of children. Probably one see-through box or cup per class and enough Smarties for one per child and a fair amount left over.

Method   Divide the school into groups. Classes work well but in a small school smaller units might be needed. You need at least four or five groups and not more than seven or eight. Keep some space between each group. A see-through cup or container is given to each group.

Get one child in each group to hold the cup (container). Pour Smarties into each cup *but . . .* one group gets loads, more than enough for all, probably two or three each; another group has about enough, perhaps a little under one each; and one group has a handful, maybe only one or two in all. This shows the principle and you adjust the cups according to number of groups. It is important to make sure that all the children see and understand that some groups have lots and some not enough.

Then ask 'Is this fair?'

Some will say 'No', if only in the groups with very little. If you are really lucky, some in the groups with lots will say 'Yes'. If this happens the response is to go over to them and, pointing to one of the groups with hardly any, say, 'Do you think it is all right for you to have all this, and for them to have so little?' If they say 'No' you have made the point. If they say 'Yes' you take their container and exchange it with the group who have almost none, so the 'haves' and the 'have nots' change over. It is very striking – and it usually gets a laugh as well!

Now ask all the children to stand up. The person with the cup in each group goes round and each child takes a Smartie (Yes – they are allowed to eat it) and once a child has taken one she/he sits down. Some groups have everyone sat down, and with Smarties over. There are other groups who have most of their members still standing because there were not enough Smarties for one each.

Pause for a moment to let this sink in.

This is the moment to become very popular with many of the children. Take the cups off groups who have Smarties over and go round the children who missed out. They can now have their Smartie and sit down. Eventually everyone has had one Smartie and there are still plenty left.

Message

Some countries, like us, have more than enough – food, water, medicine, other good things – for everyone. Others (you choose the example) have almost nothing. This is not right. Yet, as with the Smarties, if we would share better there is more than enough to go round.

Christian Aid is, at least, an attempt made by Christians to *work together* to do something about this. And Christians ought to do this because Jesus taught us to 'love our neighbours as ourselves' and that our neighbour is anyone in need. People in countries we do not know are still our neighbours, brothers and sisters. We should help them.

Prayer

Lord God,
who made us all and loves us all,
help us to share our gifts with people who have almost nothing,
so no one shall be without food, or drink, or medicine.
For Jesus' sake.
Amen.

Hymn

'When I needed a neighbour' or 'Would you walk by on the other side (Cross over the road)' or 'From heaven you came' (KS 62).

Where has Jesus gone?

This week is an Ascension assembly and next week is for Pentecost, so you may need to alter your weeks to fit (Weeks Two and Six can be used at other times).

Theme/Aim To try to help the children with what many seem to find a confusing concept (as do many adults), the Ascension.

Props *(In the bag)* A large sheet or tablecloth, coloured or opaque. Various children.

Method (A child is going to disappear from behind the sheet, in a fairly obvious way. You need to have something for them to disappear behind, either a piece of furniture (or through a door), or if the venue does not lend itself to this, stand a line of children by the sheet/cloth so the child can go behind them.)

Ask for volunteers. You need one child who will 'vanish', two more (to hold the sheet) and, if you need a human screen, as many as necessary for that (up to six, probably).

Set up the scene with those holding the sheet having one end each at floor level, and the 'victim' just behind. Announce that you are going to make him/her vanish. The sheet-holders slowly pull it up until the child behind is obscured, at which point she/he goes behind the furniture/door/children. The sheet is dropped.

'She/he is gone,' you say. 'It is magic.' Then you explain, first allowing your volunteers to go back to their places.

Ascension Day is when Jesus, who has been seen by his friends after the Resurrection, leaves again for good. The way St Luke describes it is a bit like the rather bad conjuring trick they have just seen. 'Now you see him, now you don't.' Luke is trying to show us that Jesus seemed to be no longer there to help his friends as he had before.

Message Jesus had to leave his friends or they would never have done things for themselves. Jesus was not there to do it all, but to help them learn how to live his way.

When he left they probably felt very alone, but within a short time they realised the special part of Jesus which helped them had not gone away. That discovery was made at Pentecost which we find out about next week.

Jesus' Ascension is not a trick. It was so we can become grown-up followers and choose to live the way he showed us.

Prayer

God our Father,
    we thank you for all Jesus said and did,
    and for you bringing him back from death;
    help us to see that although he left earth,
    he is still there for us when we need him.
Amen.

Hymn

Any hymn with Jesus as King is suitable. 'At the name of Jesus' and 'Rejoice, the Lord is King' are traditional hymns, while 'Jesus is Lord' is a good modern one. 'Jesus isn't dead any more' (KS 198) has really helpful words.

This assembly works equally well as the talk at an Ascension service if you should have one.

God in action

Theme/Aim This is a Pentecost assembly so you need to alter your weeks to fit. The intention is to get the children to understand that although they cannot see God, they can see God in action.

Props *(In the bag)* One electric hairdryer (and probably an extension lead so that it can be plugged in), both concealed in the bag.

(Not in the bag)
One girl with long hair.

Method Refer to Pentecost, either about to happen or just gone. Tell the children the story or, as that might make it too long, say it was the day when Jesus' followers realised that although Jesus was no longer around, God was still with them. You might add that some people say that as you can't see God, how can you know God is there? Or you might prefer to go straight into action.

Ask for a volunteer. A girl. With long hair. Bring her forward. Make her face away from the school so that her hair is visible. Plug in the hairdryer and switch on. Blow the hair. (This always seems to get a laugh.)

Now ask the question – what is making the hair move? Sooner or later someone will tell you that it is air being blown out of the hairdryer. 'Air?' you ask, innocently, 'I can't see any air.' If you can, be quite pathetic in your ignorance, examining the hairdryer, switching it on, blowing the girl's hair again, and looking at the dryer, puzzled.

'This air,' you say, 'I can't see it. How do I know that it is there?' You may get a variety of answers you can use to prolong things such as 'someone tells you the air is there' to which the reply is 'but how did they know?' In the end you will either be told, or you will have to give it them if they do not get there, 'You can't see the air but you can see what it does.'

If your chosen volunteer seems quite happy, ask her if she knew her hair was being blown. Of course she does. She knew because she could feel it move *and* she could feel the warmth. She could not see the air but she could feel the effect.

Message   You can't see God but you can see God at work, and feel God at work sometimes too. Pentecost is the coming of the Spirit to the disciples – when they became aware that the 'something' of God they had seen at work in Jesus had not gone away. Be ready to see God at work in others and feel it in yourselves.

Prayer   Father God,
  may we feel your power in our lives,
  and show it to all around us.
Amen.

Hymn   There are lots of Pentecost hymns. 'Spirit of God as strong as the wind' (sung to the tune of the Skye Boat Song) would suit well because of the wind/blowing theme. Also 'The Spirit lives to set us free' (KS 334) or 'Please fill me, Lord' (KS 282).

Note: There is an obvious possible link between the idea of God as a wind, the Pentecost story from Acts and the hairdryer. You may choose to emphasise this but there is a danger of over-complicating the assembly. One simple idea is usually best.

The man on one leg

Theme/Aim

The intention is to remind the children of the Great Commandment (Autumn Term: Week Five) in a different way *and* to show that what Jesus taught was not totally new, though it had a new slant.

Props

People with two feet. (*Yes* – if you have disabled children who cannot do this, you will either not do this assembly, or do it yourself and not use the children.)

Method

Begin by asking the children to stand up. Then show them how to stand on one leg, and then ask them to do the same. Then sit them down again, and tell them this story.

'Back in the time when Jesus first lived there was a religious teacher (they were called Rabbis). One day someone asked the Rabbi why it was so difficult to remember all the rules you needed if you were to behave well and live the right way. The Rabbi was indignant. "Difficult," he exploded. "It's not difficult at all. Why, it is so easy I could explain it all while standing on one leg."

'So he did. He stood on one leg and said, "Don't do to others what you would not like them to do to you." End of story.'

The leader now does it. Stand on one leg and say, 'Don't do to others what you would not like them to do to you.' Then, of course, you get the children to do the same thing again repeating the words with you. This ends with the words 'Feet down'.

Message

While they are still standing, though now on two feet, explain that this is quite like the second part of the Great Commandment, 'Love your neighbour as yourself'. Jesus was teaching something people had already heard and probably knew was right. The big difference is that the Rabbi on one leg was teaching in a passive way – not to do something – whereas Jesus turned it into an active thing of positively doing right. The Rabbi was still very clever in his way of teaching, and it is still a good place to begin.

Having explained it, finish by doing it again. All stand on one leg and say, 'Don't do to others what you would not like them to do to you.'

Prayer Loving Father,
  help us to care for other people not only by not hurting them,
  but also by trying to help,
  as we know you care for us.
Amen.

Hymn Anything on a caring theme. 'When I need a neighbour' has an obvious appeal. 'A man for all the people' is good (opening line 'There's a child in the streets') because the final part of the chorus is 'Help me love others too'. Others are 'Seek ye first' (KS 292) and 'Have you heard the raindrops' (KS 99).

Story – the Good Samaritan

SUMMER TERM: WEEK 7

The next two weeks do work best if done as a pair.

Theme/Aim Weeks Six, Seven and Eight are meant to develop a little more understanding of the idea 'Love your neighbour as yourself'. Week Six leads to it in, one hopes, an enjoyable way. Week Seven tells the story of the Good Samaritan, and it may be the first time some of the children will have heard it (*knowledge of even well-known Bible stories can be very scant*); Week Eight reinforces the story by acting it out.

The intention is both moral, to encourage a right way of life, and religious, to link behaviour with faith and vice versa.

Prop *(In the bag)* A Bible (the story in Luke 10:29-37) or a story-book if preferred, or even tell it from memory.

Method Have the children seated and read, or tell them, the story.

Message As Jesus needed only a few words it is most effective left with him. If you must add to it, it may be best to point out that the Samaritan would have been regarded as an enemy of the victim.

Prayer Dear God,
who made us all and loves us all,
teach us not to hate those of a different nation, colour,
or religion, but to see them as being like us,
your children, and as brother and sister
whom we should love and help if we can.
Amen.

Hymn A good one directly on the theme is 'Would you pass by on the other side' ('Cross over the road').

Act out – the Good Samaritan

As mentioned with Week Seven, that week and this work best together. One can use each separately, though to use this week on its own you do need to be sure the children know the story.

Theme/Aim See Week Seven. The hope is, by acting the story out, to 'fix' it in the minds of the children.

Props None. The children are the props. You do, however, need enough space at the front for the action to take place.

Method How you do this seems to be very much a matter of your personal style and the relationship you have with the children. The easiest way may be to read the story and for it to be acted out at each stage by the children. They do not have any words to say, their part being action only.

Begin by reminding them of the story told them the week before. It will help to refresh memories by getting the children to say what happens. (This will tend to lengthen the assembly quite a lot, however.) Then tell the children that they are going to act it out. Volunteers are needed to play a Traveller, a Priest, a Levite, a Samaritan, an Innkeeper and a number of robbers (10-12?). A child as the donkey will be popular! Then, once the recruits are in place, act it out.

The Traveller (victim) is walking along and is attacked by the robbers (this can get a bit over-vigorous at times). The robbers run off.

The Traveller is half-alive, half-dead. She/he lies on the ground. An occasional moan, perhaps?

The Priest comes along, sees the victim and goes past. (Suggest he may be worried that if he stays around it may happen to him.)

A Levite, a temple official, does the same. (Explain that had either the Priest or the Levite touched a dead body – and they may not have been sure if he was dead – they would have been regarded as contaminated and unable to carry out their religious duties.)

Then the Samaritan comes by. He is frightened by what he sees (*looks around anxiously*) but then he is so sorry for the man that he goes over to him. He helps him to his feet. He takes him to the inn (*use of donkey, optional*) and counts out money into the Innkeeper's hand to pay the bill. Then he goes on his way.

The first time this is done it tends to get very noisy and to require lots of instruction as well as the telling of the story. It is a good idea to do it again and it usually improves enormously. At the end a round of applause for the actors is much appreciated, and well deserved.

Message   See last week.

Prayer   Deliberately repeat the one used last week.

Hymn   Repeat last week (as with the prayer) to reinforce the message.

Theme/Aim   The last two weeks of the term focus on prayer. Some of the children will be leaving and it is good to leave them with the idea of being able to be in touch with God.

The aim of this assembly is to show the children that prayer is like 'talking to God', at least in part.

Props   *(In the bag)* In the bag are a letter and a telephone (a toy 'chatterphone' can be used but a real phone is better).

Method   Show the children the bag and explain that it contains some items which are to do with getting in touch or passing on a message. How do you pass on information or news or a message to someone else? (As with all cases where you ask the children questions you have to think on your feet a bit – you can't guarantee what they will say!)

In practice there are three ways to do this:

One – is to tell someone. You go up to them and say what you want to say. That is not in the bag. We carry our mouths around with us wherever we go.

Two – is to write it down and send it. A letter, a fax, the internet. A letter comes out of the bag.

Three – is by any other means of transmitting the voice – telephone, radio, tape, TV. The telephone comes out of the bag.

But there is a fourth. You will usually have to tell them this but on occasion a very bright child may work it out. *Four* – is prayer, being in touch with God. Prayer is our way of getting a message through to God. (If you have that picture of the praying hands, you could add that to the props in the bag.)

Message   As above, 'Prayer is our way of getting a message through to God', of telling him the things that matter most to us, good things as well as our needs or the people we are worried about.

(If time and the children's concentration seem to permit, add that talking to God is only one part of prayer and that we need to be silent at times and listen, so that God can be in touch with us. This depends very much on the children and your judgement on how much they will manage. It is probably better to get one part of the idea over well, that of talking to God, rather than risk losing this by putting too much in.)

Conclude by repeating 'Prayer is our way of getting a message through to God'. Then say, 'So let's do it.'

Prayer
Dear God,
   help us to know you and to be ready to tell you everything that matters to us.
Each of us has something we really want to share with you,
   and we are all going to keep very quiet now so we can think about it really hard.

Pause

Hear what we say, God,
   help us with the answer and let us know that,
   whatever happens, you are always our friend.
Amen.

Hymn
When I first did the assembly I had no idea that there was a hymn called 'Prayer is like a telephone' (KS 286). Great minds?

God is always with us

SUMMER TERM: WEEK 10

Theme/Aim This assembly is specifically directed at those children who are leaving to go on to other schools. It applies to all children, however. The assembly has the theme 'God is always with us' and the intention is to show that wherever we are God is still with us.

Props Various holiday postcards, concealed (it goes without saying?) in the bag.

Method 'I have something to show you.'

Take the cards out of the bag one by one. Pin them up if it is possible, or balance them on a ledge, or ask some children to come and hold them. What are they? Holiday postcards, of course.

Then ask the children to explain what they are. They will tell you that the cards are sent from holiday to people you know well. (This part can take quite a time especially if, as seems to help, you act a bit dumb.) Then ask them, 'When you go on holiday, do you think you go away from God?' It can be good to take a vote on it, *no* or *yes*. They will probably vote *no*!

'Quite right,' you say. 'God isn't tied to your house, or the local church, or even the vicar/priest/minister! God even comes with you when you move to a new school. When you are away, or wherever you are, God is still with you and you can talk to God – as we learned last week – through prayer.' (*If they vote* yes, *you will have to say 'Not at all' and then 'God isn't tied . . .'*)

Message God is always with you, and you can always talk to God in prayer.

Prayer It is appropriate to finish the year with the Lord's Prayer. If this is done by the Leader saying it a line at a time, with the children repeating each line after him/her, even the youngest, or those who do not know it well, can join in.

Hymn Either
Ask the leavers to choose their favourite hymn.
or
'The Journey of Life' to make the point that we are all on a continuing journey.